Presented to

_____

from

_____

On this day

_____

The

PROMISE

of PEACE

Selected Bible Verses

COMPILED BY HOPE CLARKE

A DayMaker Greeting Book

Peace

Throughout His Word, God offers His children many promises—among them, the promise of peace.

May these one hundred carefully selected Scriptures lighten your heart and quiet your soul. May they remind you of God's awesome presence in your life—and the peace that only He can provide.

BLESSED

PEAC

ARE THE

EMAKERS,

for they will be

called sons of God.

MATTHEW 5:9

For he himself is our peace,
who has made the two one
and has destroyed the barrier,
the dividing wall of hostility,
by abolishing in his flesh the law
with its commandments and regulations.
His purpose was to create in himself
one new man out of the two,
thus making peace, and in this one body
to reconcile both of them to God
through the cross, by which
he put to death their hostility.

EPHESIANS 2:14-16

For the kingdom of God is not
a matter of eating and drinking,
but of righteousness, peace
and joy in the Holy Spirit.

ROMANS 14:17

Therefore, since we have been made right
in God's sight by faith, we have peace with God
because of what Jesus Christ our Lord
has done for us.

ROMANS 5:1 NLT

"I have told you these things,
so that in me you may have peace.
In this world you will have trouble.
But take heart! I have overcome the world."

JOHN 16:33

"If a man of peace is there,
your peace will rest on him;
if not, it will return to you."

LUKE 10:6

"Peace I leave with you; my peace I give you.
I do not give to you as the world gives.
Do not let your hearts be troubled
and do not be afraid."

JOHN 14:27

The fruit of righteousness
will be peace;
the effect of righteousness
will be quietness
and confidence forever.

ISAIAH 32:17

For God is not a God of disorder but of peace.

1 CORINTHIANS 14:33

Look at
those who
are honest
and good,
for A
WONDERFUL
FUTURE
lies before those
who love peace.

PSALM 37:37 NLT

He came and preached peace
to you who were far away
and peace to those who were near.
For through him we both have access
to the Father by one Spirit.

EPHESIANS 2:17-18

Whatever you have learned or received
or heard from me, or seen in me—
put it into practice.
And the God of peace will be with you.

PHILIPPIANS 4:9

Hold them in the highest regard in love
because of their work.
Live in peace with each other.

I THESSALONIANS 5:13

Make every effort to live in peace
with all men and to be holy;
without holiness no one will see the Lord.

HEBREWS 12:14

For the Scriptures say,
"If you want a happy life and good days,
keep your tongue from speaking evil,
and keep your lips from telling lies.
Turn away from evil and do good.
Work hard at living in peace with others."

1 PETER 3:10-11 NLT

But this is what you must do:
Tell the truth to each other.
Render verdicts in your courts
that are just and that lead to peace.

ZECHARIAH 8:16 NLT

If your sinful nature controls your mind,
there is death. But if the Holy Spirit
controls your mind, there is life and peace.

ROMANS 8:6 NLT

Deceit is in the heart
of those who devise evil,
but counselors of peace have joy.

PROVERBS 12:20 NKJV

Let the peace of Christ
rule in your hearts,
since as members of one body
you were called to peace.
And be thankful.

COLOSSIANS 3:15

Turn away from evil and do good.
Work hard at living in peace with others.

If only you had
paid attention to my commands,
your peace would have been like a river,
your righteousness
like the waves of the sea.

ISAIAH 48:18

PEACE LIKE A RIVER

"May the LORD show you his favor
and give you his peace.'"

NUMBERS 6:26 NLT

I will listen to what God the LORD will say;
he promises peace to his people, his saints—
but let them not return to folly.

PSALM 85:8

The LORD gives strength to his people;
the LORD blesses his people with peace.

PSALM 29:11

"Though the mountains be shaken and the hills
be removed, yet my unfailing love for you will not
be shaken nor my covenant of peace be removed,"
says the LORD, who has compassion on you.

ISAIAH 54:10

"'I will grant peace in the land,
and you will lie down
and no one will make you afraid.
I will remove savage beasts from the land,
and the sword will not pass
through your country.'"

LEVITICUS 26:6

When you march up to attack a city,
make its people an offer of peace.

DEUTERONOMY 20:10

Now may the Lord of peace himself
give you peace at all times and in every way.
The Lord be with all of you.

2 THESSALONIANS 3:16

Jesus said to the woman,
"Your faith has saved you; go in peace."

LUKE 7:50

Then Joshua made a treaty of peace
with them to let them live,
and the leaders of the assembly
ratified it by oath.

JOSHUA 9:15

But the LORD said to him, "Peace!
Do not be afraid. You are not going to die."

JUDGES 6:23

So Gideon built an altar to the LORD there
and called it The LORD is Peace. To this day
it stands in Ophrah of the Abiezrites.

JUDGES 6:24

"Creating praise on the lips of the mourners
in Israel. Peace, peace, to those far and near,"
says the LORD. "And I will heal them."

ISAIAH 57:19

But the meek shall inherit the earth,
and shall delight themselves
in the abundance of peace.

PSALM 37:11 NKJV

I WILL
LIE DOWN
AND SLEEP
IN PEACE,
FOR YOU
ALONE,
O LORD,
MAKE ME
DWELL
IN SAFETY.

PSALM 4:8

Discipline your son,
and he will give you peace;
he will bring delight to your soul.

PROVERBS 29:17

When a man's ways
are pleasing to the LORD,
he makes even his enemies
live at peace with him.

PROVERBS 16:7

But the wisdom that comes from God
is first of all pure; then peace-loving,
considerate, submissive, full of mercy
and good fruit, impartial and sincere.

JAMES 3:17

You will keep in perfect peace
him whose mind is steadfast,
because he trusts in you.

ISAIAH 26:3

"If the home is deserving,
let your peace rest on it; if it is not,
let your peace return to you."

MATTHEW 10:13

"Salt is good,
but if it loses its saltiness,
how can you make it salty again?
Have salt in yourselves,
and be at peace with each other."

MARK 9:50

Let us therefore make every effort
to do what leads to peace
and to mutual edification.

ROMANS 14:19

Finally, brothers, good-by.
Aim for perfection, listen to my appeal,
be of one mind, live in peace.
And the God of love and peace
will be with you.

2 CORINTHIANS 13:11

The PEACE

of GOD

Be with You

Always

But the fruit of the Spirit is love,
joy, peace, patience, kindness, goodness,
faithfulness, gentleness and self-control.
Against such things there is no law.

GALATIANS 5:22-23

Be completely humble and gentle;
be patient, bearing with one another in love.
Make every effort to keep the unity
of the Spirit through the bond of peace.

EPHESIANS 4:2-3

Flee the evil desires of youth,
and pursue righteousness, faith, love and peace,
along with those who call on the Lord
out of a pure heart.

2 TIMOTHY 2:22

Remind the people to be subject to rulers
and authorities, to be obedient, to be ready
to do whatever is good, to slander no one,
to be peaceable and considerate, and to
show true humility toward all men.

TITUS 3:1-2

Great peace have they who love your law,
and nothing can make them stumble.

PSALM 119:165

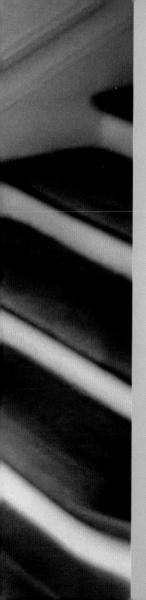

"When
you enter
a house,
first say,
'PEACE
TO THIS
HOUSE.'"

LUKE 10:5

Grace and peace
be yours in abundance
through the knowledge of God
and of Jesus our Lord.

2 PETER 1:2

Grace, mercy and peace from God the Father
and from Jesus Christ, the Father's Son,
will be with us in truth and love.

2 JOHN 1:3

Praise the LORD, O Jerusalem!
Praise your God, O Zion!
For he has fortified the bars of your gates
and blessed your children within you.
He sends peace across your nation
and satisfies you with plenty
of the finest wheat.

PSALM 147:12-14 NLT

If you do this,
you will experience God's peace,
which is far more wonderful than
the human mind can understand.
His peace will guard your hearts and
minds as you live in Christ Jesus.

PHILIPPIANS 4:7 NLT

A dry crust eaten in peace
is better than a great feast with strife.

PROVERBS 17:1 NLT

May God himself, the God of peace,
sanctify you through and through.
May your whole spirit, soul and body
be kept blameless at the coming
of our Lord Jesus Christ.

1 THESSALONIANS 5:23

"May there be peace within your walls
and security within your citadels."

PSALM 122:7

May the God of hope fill you
with all joy and peace as you trust in him,
so that you may overflow with hope
by the power of the Holy Spirit.

ROMANS 15:13

If a wise man contends with a foolish man,
whether the fool rages or laughs,
there is no peace.

PROVERBS 29:9 NKJV

A heart at peace gives life to the body,
but envy rots the bones.

PROVERBS 14:30

"Submit to God and be at peace with him;
in this way prosperity will come to you."

JOB 22:21

My People
will Live in
Peaceful
Dwelling Places,

in secure homes,

in undisturbed

places of rest.

ISAIAH 32:18

A time to love and a time to hate,
a time for war and a time for peace.

ECCLESIASTES 3:8

"'Nevertheless,
I will bring health and healing to it;
I will heal my people and will let them
enjoy abundant peace and security.'"

JEREMIAH 33:6

All the lands are at rest and at peace;
they break into singing.

ISAIAH 14:7

LORD, you establish peace for us;
all that we have accomplished
you have done for us.

ISAIAH 26:12

"Glory to God in the highest,
and on earth peace to men
on whom his favor rests."

LUKE 2:14

"All your sons will be taught by the LORD,
and great will be your children's peace."

ISAIAH 54:13

"Come unto me, all who are weary
and burdeded, and I will give you rest."

MATTHEW 11:28

Then he said to her,
"Daughter, your faith has healed you.
Go in peace."

LUKE 8:48

"Blessed is the king who comes
in the name of the Lord!"
"Peace in heaven and glory in the highest!"

LUKE 19:38

While they were still talking about this,
Jesus himself stood among them
and said to them, "Peace be with you."

LUKE 24:36

On the evening of that first day of the week,
when the disciples were together,
with the doors locked for fear of the Jews,
Jesus came and stood among them and said,
"Peace be with you!"

JOHN 20:19

Grace and peace to you from God our Father
and the Lord Jesus Christ.

1 CORINTHIANS 1:3

Again Jesus said, "Peace be with you!
As the Father has sent me, I am sending you."

JOHN 20:21

If it is
possible,
as far as
it depends
on you,
LIVE AT
PEACE with
everyone.

ROMANS 12:18

You know the message
God sent to the people of Israel,
telling the good news of peace
through Jesus Christ,
who is Lord of all.

ACTS 10:36

But glory, honor and peace
for everyone who does good:
first for the Jew, then for the Gentile.

ROMANS 2:10

"There is no peace," says the LORD, "for the wicked."

ISAIAH 48:22

The God of peace will soon
crush Satan under your feet.
The grace of our Lord Jesus be with you.

ROMANS 16:20

The God of peace be with you all. Amen.

ROMANS 15:33

No discipline seems pleasant at the time,
but painful. Later on, however, it produces
a harvest of righteousness and peace
for those who have been trained by it.

HEBREWS 12:11

"Or else let them come to me for refuge;
let them make peace with me,
Yes, let them make peace with me."

ISAIAH 27:5

Peace and mercy to all who follow this rule,
even to the Israel of God.

GALATIANS 6:16

Grace and peace to you from God our Father
and the Lord Jesus Christ.

2 CORINTHIANS 1:2

Stand firm then, with the belt of truth
buckled around your waist, with the breastplate
of righteousness in place, and with your feet
fitted with the readiness that comes from
the gospel of peace.

EPHESIANS 6:14-15

For God was pleased to have all his fullness
dwell in him, and through him to reconcile
to himself all things, whether things on earth
or things in heaven, by making peace
through his blood, shed on the cross.

COLOSSIANS 1:19-20

I urge, then, first of all, that requests,
prayers, intercession and thanksgiving
be made for everyone—
for kings and all those in authority,
that we may live peaceful and quiet lives
in all godliness and holiness.

I TIMOTHY 2:1-2

Peacemakers who sow in peace
raise a harvest of righteousness.

JAMES 3:18

YOU WILL GO OUT IN JOY

and be led forth in peace;

the mountains and hills

will burst into song before you,

and all the trees of the field

will clap their hands.

ISAIAH 55:12

So then, dear friends,
since you are looking forward to this,
make every effort to be found spotless,
blameless and at peace with him.

2 PETER 3:14

May the God of peace,
who through the blood of the eternal covenant
brought back from the dead our Lord Jesus,
that great Shepherd of the sheep,
equip you with everything good for doing his will,
and may he work in us what is pleasing to him,
through Jesus Christ, to whom
be glory for ever and ever.
Amen.

HEBREWS 13:20-21

Greet one another with a kiss of love.
Peace to all of you who are in Christ.

1 PETER 5:14

But those who turn to crooked ways
the LORD will banish with the evildoers.
Peace be upon Israel.

PSALM 125:5

Of the increase of his government
and peace there will be no end.
He will reign on David's throne
and over his kingdom, establishing and
upholding it with justice and righteousness
from that time on and forever.
The zeal of the LORD Almighty
will accomplish this.

ISAIAH 9:7

For the sake of my brothers and friends,
I will say, "Peace be within you."

PSALM 122:8

But if the unbeliever leaves, let him do so.
A believing man or woman is not bound in such
circumstances; God has called us to live in peace.

1 CORINTHIANS 7:15

For to us a child is born, to us a son is given,
and the government will be on his shoulders.
And he will be called Wonderful Counselor,
Mighty God, Everlasting Father, Prince of Peace.

ISAIAH 9:6

Look upon Zion, the city of our festivals;
your eyes will see Jerusalem, a peaceful abode,
a tent that will not be moved;
its stakes will never be pulled up,
nor any of its ropes broken.

ISAIAH 33:20

Peace to the brothers, and love with faith
from God the Father and the Lord Jesus Christ.

EPHESIANS 6:23

Mercy, peace and love
be yours in abundance.

JUDE 1:2

GREETING BOOKS

ISBN 1-58660-817-7

Cover images: © Daniel Proctor/Kamil Vajnar (Photonica)

Published by Barbour Books, an imprint of Barbour Publishing, Inc.
P.O. Box 719, Uhrichsville, Ohio 44683, www.barbourbooks.com

Member of the
Evangelical Christian
Publishers Association

Printed in China

5 4 3 2 1